Goodman's Five-Star ACTIVITY BOOKS

Test-Taker Practice Series

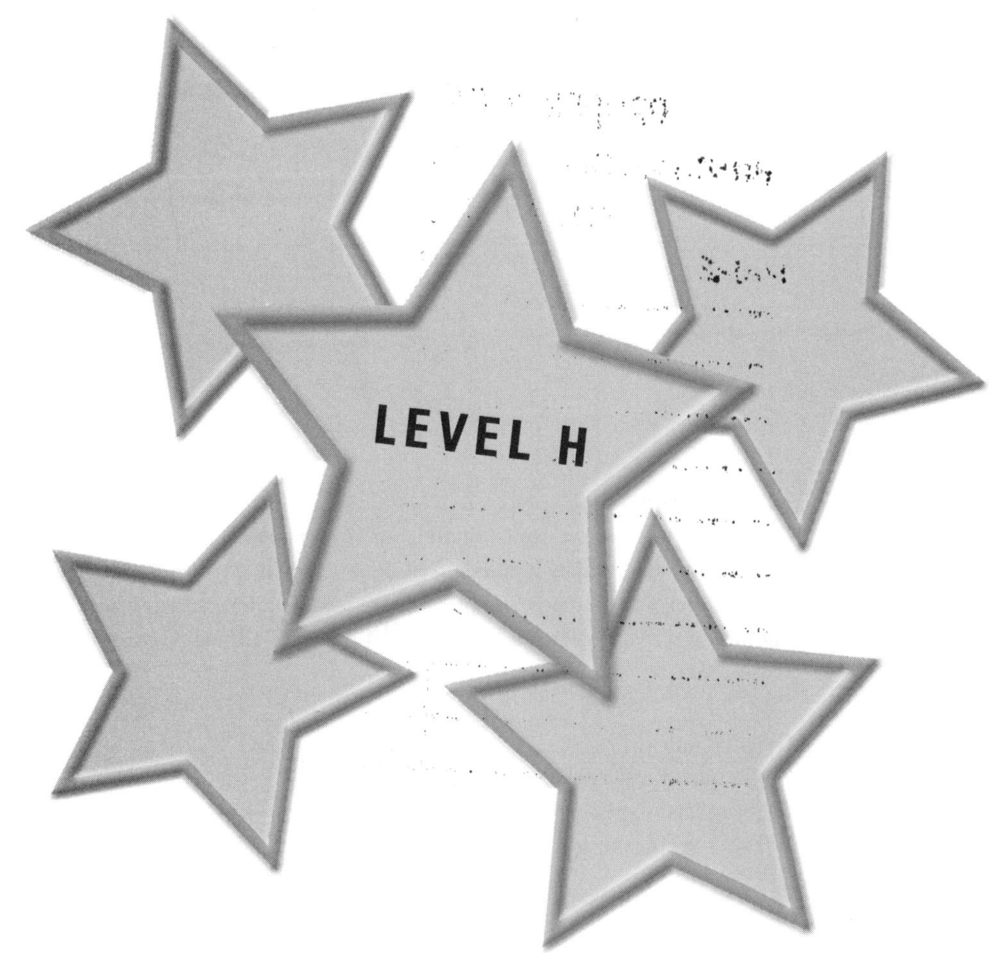

Burton Goodman

JAMESTOWN PUBLISHERS
a division of NTC/Contemporary Publishing Group
Lincolnwood, Illinois USA

Acknowledgments
"New Mexico Nocturne" and "Autumn Dusk" by Manuela Williams Crosno. © 1988 by Manuela Williams Crosno. Used by permission of the author's agent, Burton Goodman.
Stories, articles, adaptations, and other instructional materials by Burton Goodman.
The author wishes to express profound gratitude to Matthew Goodman for his invaluable assistance.

Cover Design
Karen Christoffersen
Interior Illustrations
Other Brother Design

ISBN: 0-8092-0352-9
Published by Jamestown Publishers,
a division of NTC/Contemporary Publishing Group, Inc.,
4255 West Touhy Avenue,
Lincolnwood (Chicago), Illinois, 60712-1975, U.S.A.

Manufactured in the United States of America.

01 02 03 04 MN 10 9 8 7 6 5 4 3 2

CONTENTS

ABOUT THE SERIES

Goodman's Five-Star Activity Books, Level H reinforces and extends the exercises and literary themes in *Conflicts* and *More Conflicts* in *Goodman's Five-Star Stories*, Level H. This activity book can be used in conjunction with *Conflicts* and *More Conflicts*, or it can be used on a completely independent basis.

Goodman's Five-Star Activity Books
Test-Taker Practice Series

The *Goodman's Five-Star Activity Books* series has been specially designed to help students master the kinds of exercises most frequently found on standardized tests. The series uses high-quality multicultural nonfiction and fiction materials to familiarize students with the kinds of questions they are likely to encounter. At the same time, the books offer students numerous opportunities to improve their language arts skills and their test scores through practice.

Each book in the series focuses on developing skills and competencies in reading comprehension, mechanics, and writing. Provision is also made for study skills practice.

The **Reading Comprehension** section provides students with 10 standardized questions with an emphasis on critical thinking and vocabulary. The **Mechanics** section offers repeated practice in capitalization, punctuation, the comma, spelling, and grammar. The **Writing** section requires students to respond to a wide variety of specific and open-ended writing tasks.

The series includes an attractive Test-Taker self-scoring feature that enables students to score and record their results.

Used along with the books in *Goodman's Five-Star Stories*, or on an independent basis, I feel certain that the *Goodman's Five-Star Activity Books* will help students develop the confidence and competency to improve their test scores. In addition, the books will help readers master many of the essential language arts skills they need for success in school and in life.

Burton Goodman

DIRECTIONS
Read the article. Then answer the questions that follow.

Dangerous Animals: Land, Sea, and Air

The world of nature can be a very dangerous place. However, it is hardly as dangerous for human beings as it is for other animals. The reason for this is that human beings live at the top of the food chain. That means no other animals hunt us as prey.

Compare our existence, for example, with the perilous life of wild pigs in the jungles of Central America. They must constantly be on the lookout for a hungry jaguar. Consider, too, the life of a turtle, a seal, or a small fish in a tropical ocean where the tiger shark relentlessly hunts for its next meal. Tiger sharks are so ravenous that they are often caught with license plates, shoes, and even paint cans in their stomachs!

Even though we are not hunted by other animals, there are plenty of creatures on land, in the sea, and in the air that we would hate to encounter on a dark night—or, for that matter, at any other time.

Since we spend most of our time on land, we have been warned about dangerous land animals like the black bear. Clearly, we would not want to confront one, but the black bear is apparently less violent than we might imagine. Some studies suggest that, usually, the worst thing black bears do is chase human beings, and that most of the time if people just shout at the bear it will "turn tail" and run. Still, the black bear *is* unpredictable and *can* be very dangerous, so it certainly is advisable to stay out of its way and not antagonize it.

For additional exercises and a theme-related story about the most dangerous animal of all, see "The Most Dangerous Game" in *Conflicts* in *Goodman's Five-Star Stories,* Level H.

Although the black bear is frightening and huge, it is as meek as a kitten compared with a very different and far more dangerous land animal—the spitting cobra. This snake lives in central Africa. It usually grows to a length of five to six feet and is tan to black in color. Why is it called the spitting cobra? The answer immediately becomes apparent to any creature that has the misfortune to meet it.

When the spitting cobra is disturbed, it rears up off the ground and ejects a stream of poison, called venom, from holes in the front of its head. The snake aims for the enemy's eyes, and from seven feet away or less, the spitting cobra almost never misses. The venom

temporarily blinds the victim, rendering it helpless to the cobra's sharp fangs.

Fortunately, it's not very likely that we will ever happen across the path of a spitting cobra. However, dangers in the animal world are not limited to the land. Plenty of dangerous creatures inhabit the water.

One of these is the piranha, a fierce little fish that has razor-sharp teeth. Piranhas are found in the Amazon River in South America. They sometimes travel in groups, or schools, of 1,000 or more, and they can strip the flesh from a victim in just a few seconds.

There are many terrifying tales about piranhas, and some of these stories are indeed true. For example, there are instances in which piranhas have devoured cattle that have wandered into the river. Interestingly, piranhas only attack when blood is already in the water, so they usually limit their attacks to animals that are already wounded. In fact, certain Indian tribes in the Amazon region regularly swim with piranhas, and they are ignored by the fish.

Our fate will be far worse, however, if we are unlucky enough to step on a stonefish, a spiny fish that lives near the coral reefs off the coast of Australia. The poison from a stonefish's spikes causes death within hours if the victim is not treated at once with a powerful antidote.

Just as dangerous as the stonefish is the moray eel, a long, snakelike fish found in tropical seas. The moray eel has a very large head, strong jaws, and a mouth filled with sharp, pointy teeth that it uses to inflict severe bites on its victims. The flesh of most moray eels is poisonous, and any enemy that bites the moray suffers a painful and speedy death.

Surprisingly, the moray eel is not poisonous if it is *cooked* before it is eaten. During ancient Roman times, the moray eel was considered a prized delicacy. It is said that the Roman emperor Julius Caesar had 5,000 of them served at one of his banquets.

Remarkably, none of these land or sea creatures is nearly as dangerous to human beings as an animal that lives in the air. It is a creature so small that people sometimes do not even notice it—it is the mosquito.

Mosquitoes are among the world's oldest creatures. It is believed that mosquitoes have existed on earth for more than 100 million years. They have been biting people ever since the days of cave people. The mosquito is also one of the most common insects in the world; there are about 3,000 different species.

Of course, most mosquitoes are nothing more than a nuisance as they buzz around us when we try to fall asleep. However, some species of mosquitoes that live in the tropics are carriers of malaria, an extremely dangerous disease. The mosquitoes transmit malaria into the bloodstream of the people they bite. Every year, millions of new cases of malaria are reported. More than a million people around the world die each year from illnesses carried by mosquitoes. In fact, more people have died from diseases carried by mosquitoes than have died in *all* the wars in history.

Researchers continue to find new, stronger drugs to treat malaria, and scientists are trying to find ways to control mosquitoes that carry disease. However, the current experiments are still far from successful. For now, the most dangerous creature in the world is one of the smallest—the mosquito.

Go on ➤

I. Reading Comprehension Skills

Fill in the circle next to the correct answer.

1. What is the main purpose of the article?
   - Ⓐ to warn the reader about the risks of confronting a spitting cobra.
   - Ⓑ to encourage research into ways to control mosquitoes that transmit disease.
   - Ⓒ to provide information about a variety of dangerous animals.
   - Ⓓ to make the reader aware that stepping on a stonefish can produce deadly results.

2. Which one of the following does the article suggest?
   - Ⓐ Studies indicate that none of the terrifying stories about piranhas are true.
   - Ⓑ Although black bears are large, they are actually friendly creatures that need not be avoided.
   - Ⓒ Scientists believe that malaria will shortly cease to be a significant problem.
   - Ⓓ Human beings are fortunate to live at the top of the food chain.

3. Why should an enemy avoid biting a moray eel?
   - Ⓐ Moray eels are beneficial to nature and should never be attacked.
   - Ⓑ The flesh of most moray eels is poisonous.
   - Ⓒ The moray eel's flesh is so tough that the eel is not likely to be injured.
   - Ⓓ A moray eel's flesh is razor-sharp to the touch.

4. It is correct to infer that
   - Ⓐ tiger sharks will eat just about anything.
   - Ⓑ all mosquitoes carry dangerous diseases.
   - Ⓒ piranhas are unlikely to attack a wounded animal that is very large.
   - Ⓓ Most animals are defenseless and are unable to protect themselves.

5. An interesting point the article makes is that
   - Ⓐ antidotes can be effective for treating victims who have been poisoned.
   - Ⓑ hungry jaguars pose a threat to animals around them.
   - Ⓒ a tiny insect can be extraordinarily dangerous.
   - Ⓓ no dangerous animals live in the sea.

Answers

1.	Ⓐ	Ⓑ	Ⓒ	Ⓓ
2.	Ⓐ	Ⓑ	Ⓒ	Ⓓ
3.	Ⓐ	Ⓑ	Ⓒ	Ⓓ
4.	Ⓐ	Ⓑ	Ⓒ	Ⓓ
5.	Ⓐ	Ⓑ	Ⓒ	Ⓓ

Go on ➤

6. Which statement is *not* true?
   Ⓐ Sooner or later, most people will cross the path of a spitting cobra.
   Ⓑ Piranhas sometimes travel in schools of 1,000 or more.
   Ⓒ Moray eels have very sharp teeth.
   Ⓓ The mosquito is one of the most common insects in the world.

7. Which word best expresses the tone of the article?
   Ⓐ humorous
   Ⓑ serious
   Ⓒ sad
   Ⓓ suspenseful

8. The tiger shark is especially dangerous because it relentlessly hunts its prey. The word *relentlessly* means
   Ⓐ intelligently.
   Ⓑ slowly or cautiously.
   Ⓒ cheerfully or happily.
   Ⓓ without pity.

9. Tiger sharks are so ravenous that they will eat license plates and shoes. The word *ravenous* means
   Ⓐ very hungry.
   Ⓑ fearless.
   Ⓒ swift.
   Ⓓ stupid.

10. The article advises the reader to avoid the black bear and not to antagonize it. The word *antagonize* means
   Ⓐ to take pictures of.
   Ⓑ to feed.
   Ⓒ to annoy or make an enemy of.
   Ⓓ to help or assist.

Answers				
6.	Ⓐ	Ⓑ	Ⓒ	Ⓓ
7.	Ⓐ	Ⓑ	Ⓒ	Ⓓ
8.	Ⓐ	Ⓑ	Ⓒ	Ⓓ
9.	Ⓐ	Ⓑ	Ⓒ	Ⓓ
10.	Ⓐ	Ⓑ	Ⓒ	Ⓓ

How many questions did you answer correctly? Circle your score below. Then fill in your **Comprehension** score on the **Test-Taker Score Chart** on the inside of the back cover.

Number Correct	1	2	3	4	5	6	7	8	9	10
My Score	10	20	30	40	50	60	70	80	90	100

Go on ➤

II. Mechanics (capitalization, punctuation, the comma, spelling, and grammar)

Fill in the circle next to the correct answer.

1. Which sentence has an error in capitalization?
   Ⓐ The stonefish lives near the coral reefs off the coast of Australia.
   Ⓑ The spitting cobra lives in central Africa.
   Ⓒ Certain indian tribes swim with piranhas in the Amazon River.
   Ⓓ During Roman times, Julius Caesar ate moray eels at banquets.

2. Which sentence is not punctuated correctly?
   Ⓐ Tiger sharks eat turtles, seals fish and even other sharks.
   Ⓑ The poison from a stonefish's spikes can cause death within hours.
   Ⓒ Did you know that some mosquitoes transmit malaria?
   Ⓓ There are many terrifying stories about piranhas, and some of the stories are true.

3. Which sentence needs a comma or does not use the comma correctly?
   Ⓐ Mosquitoes are quite small, but some of them can be deadly.
   Ⓑ The moray eel, a long snakelike fish lives in tropical waters.
   Ⓒ Not all mosquitoes, of course, transmit malaria.
   Ⓓ However, some mosquitoes are carriers of deadly diseases.

4. Which sentence has an error in spelling in the underlined word?
   Ⓐ Do you find it <u>surprising</u> that mosquitoes can be so deadly?
   Ⓑ The piranha is a small fish <u>whose</u> teeth are razor-sharp.
   Ⓒ Some experiments to control mosquitoes were not <u>sucessful</u>.
   Ⓓ The spitting cobra <u>usually</u> grows to a length of five to six feet.

5. Which sentence has an error in grammar?
   Ⓐ Piranhas can kill their victims in just a few seconds.
   Ⓑ Mosquitoes are among the world's oldest creatures.
   Ⓒ Witnesses saw the shark attack its victim.
   Ⓓ Millions of new cases of malaria is reported each year.

Answers				
1.	Ⓐ	Ⓑ	Ⓒ	Ⓓ
2.	Ⓐ	Ⓑ	Ⓒ	Ⓓ
3.	Ⓐ	Ⓑ	Ⓒ	Ⓓ
4.	Ⓐ	Ⓑ	Ⓒ	Ⓓ
5.	Ⓐ	Ⓑ	Ⓒ	Ⓓ

How many questions did you answer correctly? Circle your score below. Then fill in your **Mechanics** score on the **Test-Taker Score Chart** on the inside of the back cover.

Number Correct	1	2	3	4	5
Your Score	20	40	60	80	100

Go on ➤

III. Writing

Answer the questions that follow. You may look back at the article as often as you wish.

1. Read the statement below.

   The world of nature is hardly as dangerous for human beings as it is for other animals.

   Use examples and details from the article to support this statement.

2. On the lines below, explain how *three* of the animals discussed in the article are able to poison their victims.

   Three animals that can poison their victims are

Go on ➤

3. Use the chart below to compare and contrast the piranha and the moray eel. List how are they similar and how they are different.

The Piranha and the Moray Eel	
How are they similar?	How are they different?

4. On the lines below, compare the piranha and the moray eel. Use the notes you wrote on the chart above to help you organize your writing.

Go on ➤

5. Complete the chart below by listing five facts about mosquitoes.

Facts About Mosquitoes

1. ______________________________

2. ______________________________

3. ______________________________

4. ______________________________

5. ______________________________

6. Now write a short essay entitled "The Amazing Mosquito." In your essay include the facts listed on the chart.

The Amazing Mosquito

____

____

____

____

____

____

____

____

____

____

____

____

____

Go on ➤

7. The article states that "there are plenty of creatures on land, in the sea, and in the air that we would hate to encounter. . . ." Keeping this in mind, write the beginning of a short story with the title below. Use each of the words in the box in your story.

amazing	**distance**	**startled**	**noticed**
suddenly	**swiftly**	**attempted**	**scary**

A Jungle Adventure

DIRECTIONS

Read the story. Then answer the questions that follow.

A Horsey Name

based on a story by Anton Chekhov

Major-General Kurlov was suffering from a terrible toothache. He had tried everything he could think of to cure it. He had rinsed his mouth with lemon juice and vinegar, had taken two kinds of medicine, and had put cotton balls soaked in rubbing alcohol into his ears. All these remedies, however, failed to relieve the severe pain the general was experiencing.

He finally sent for the dentist. The dentist investigated the general's mouth with great care. He picked and poked at tooth and gum, and finally announced, "The tooth is too far gone to be saved and must be removed."

"Absolutely not!" shouted the general. "I had a tooth pulled once, and it was the worst experience of my life! I was in bed for a week! I forbid you to even think about pulling my tooth!"

After the dentist left, everyone in the house began to offer General Kurlov suggestions for possible remedies. Finally, his personal servant, a young man named Ivan, came to him with advice.

"Your Excellency," he said, "I know a man in the town of Sarloff who can help you with your toothache."

"Is that so?" said the general doubtfully. "And who might this man be?"

"He is a dentist like no other. He has . . . well you can say he has a *gift* for dentistry. All he has to do is wave his hands in front of your face, and your pain disappears. He just waves his hands back

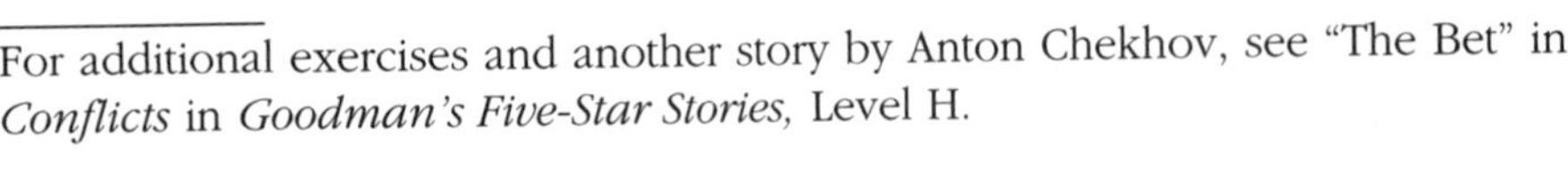

For additional exercises and another story by Anton Chekhov, see "The Bet" in *Conflicts* in *Goodman's Five-Star Stories,* Level H.

and forth and no more pain! The people in Sarloff have him come to their homes, but he cures people in other cities by telegraph. All you have to do, your Excellency, is send him a telegram. Say, 'I, Major-General Alexei Kurlov, have a toothache. I would like you to cure it.' You can send him his fee by mail."

"That's nonsense," sputtered the general. "It's ridiculous! It's nothing but humbug!"

"Oh, do send him a telegram, Alexei," begged the general's wife. "I know you don't believe it will do you any good but, after all, what harm can it do?"

"Very well, then," the general finally consented. "Ouch! I cannot stand this anymore. Come on, Ivan, where does your man live? What is his name?"

"He is known to everyone in Sarloff," said the servant. "Just address the telegram to Mr. Jacob . . . Jacob . . ."

"Yes? Come on, man. Time is wasting!"

"Jacob . . .Jacob . . . I can't remember his last name. Jacob . . . what is his name? I knew it just a few minutes ago. Let me think."

Ivan raised his eyes to the ceiling and moved his lips. Kurlov and his wife waited impatiently for him to remember the name. "Well, what is it?" the general finally asked gruffly.

"Just one more minute! Jacob . . . Jacob . . . I can't remember it! It's a common name too. Something to do with a horse. Wait a second . . . is it Colt? Colton? No, those aren't right. I know perfectly well it's a horsey name, but it has gone completely out of my head!"

"A horsey name?" said the general. "Mare? Maresden, Maresfield? Mariweather?"

"No, no. Hold on. Horse . . . Horsley . . ."

"Horston?" suggested the general's wife. "Hurston, perhaps?"

"No, it isn't either of those . . . just a second . . . Trotter? No . . . it's not Trotter."

"How am I to send that telegram? Think a little harder!"

"One moment! Gallup . . . Stable . . . Stapleton . . ."

"Ryder?" said the general. "Come on now, is it Ryder?"

"No, no . . . I've forgotten it!"

"Then why on earth did you come pestering me with your advice if you can't remember the man's name?" shouted the general. "Get out of here!"

Ivan slowly left the room as the general clutched his cheek and stormed through the house. "Ouch!" he howled. "I'm blind, blind with pain!"

Shortly afterward the servant was again summoned by the general. "Well, have you thought of it?" the general asked.

The servant shook his head sadly.

An hour later Ivan was sent for again. "Is it Pacer?" the general asked. "Stallworth?"

"No, no," answered Ivan and, casting up his eyes, he went on thinking aloud.

Evening came and still the name had not been found. The general did not sleep a wink but paced, groaning, back and forth in his room. At three in the morning he went out and tapped at the servant's window. "It isn't Barnes, is it?" he asked, almost in tears.

"No, not Barnes, your Excellency," said Ivan apologetically.

"Is it Farmer?" How about Herd? Is it Herder?"

Ivan shook his head no.

"What an abominable memory you have! That name is worth more than anything on earth to me now. I'm in agony, I tell you!"

The next morning the general sent for the dentist again. "I'll have it out!" he cried. "I can't stand this any longer!"

The dentist pulled the aching tooth, and soon the general's pain subsided. Having done his work, the dentist climbed into his carriage and drove away. In the field just outside the front gate, he met Ivan. Judging from the deep wrinkles that furrowed his brow, Ivan was racking his brain about something. "Steed . . . Steedman . . . Bronco . . . Brockman . . ."

"Hello, Ivan," cried the dentist as he drove up. "Would you mind selling me a load of hay. I need . . ."

"*Hay!*" Ivan exclaimed. He threw up his arms and rushed toward the house as if a mad dog were after him. "I've thought of the name, your Excellency!" Ivan shrieked with delight as he burst into the general's study. "*Hayes*! Hayes is the man's name! Send a telegram to *Hayes*!"

"It's too late now!" answered the general with scorn. "I don't need your horsey name anymore. Now go away—and stop nagging me!"

Go on ➤

I. Reading Comprehension Skills

Fill in the circle next to the correct answer.

1. What is the story mostly about?
   - Ⓐ good ways to get rid of a toothache
   - Ⓑ the life of Major-General Alexei Kurlov
   - Ⓒ a servant's attempts to remember the name of a very unusual dentist
   - Ⓓ the pain caused by a terrible toothache

2. We may infer that the general was reluctant to have the tooth pulled because he
   - Ⓐ thought the tooth would eventually get better.
   - Ⓑ did not have confidence in his dentist.
   - Ⓒ did not think it was possible to extract the tooth.
   - Ⓓ suffered a great deal the last time he had a tooth pulled.

3. Ivan finally realized that the dentist's name was Hayes when
   - Ⓐ he saw a load of hay in the barn.
   - Ⓑ the general cried out, "Hey, what are you doing?"
   - Ⓒ the dentist mentioned that he needed a load of hay.
   - Ⓓ he noticed a haze settling over the field.

4. Which statement is true?
   - Ⓐ The story relies strongly on the use of words associated with horses.
   - Ⓑ Ivan remembered the dentist's name just in time.
   - Ⓒ General Kurlov acted pleasantly throughout the story.
   - Ⓓ The general greatly appreciated his servant's efforts.

5. The pun, or "play on words," in the last line of the story is based on the fact that
   - Ⓐ the words "go away," sound like "neigh."
   - Ⓑ the servant thought of the dentist's name at the last minute, so the horse finished last.
   - Ⓒ the general didn't need a "horsey name" because he was "hoarse" from crying out in pain from the toothache.
   - Ⓓ the general told the servant to stop "nagging" him, and a "nag" is a horse.

Answers				
1.	Ⓐ	Ⓑ	Ⓒ	Ⓓ
2.	Ⓐ	Ⓑ	Ⓒ	Ⓓ
3.	Ⓐ	Ⓑ	Ⓒ	Ⓓ
4.	Ⓐ	Ⓑ	Ⓒ	Ⓓ
5.	Ⓐ	Ⓑ	Ⓒ	Ⓓ

Go on ➤

6. What was the author's main purpose in writing the story?
   Ⓐ to provide valuable information
   Ⓑ to entertain the reader
   Ⓒ to change the reader's mind
   Ⓓ to make the reader feel sad

7. Which one of the following best describes the story?
   Ⓐ tragic
   Ⓑ solemn
   Ⓒ highly suspenseful
   Ⓓ amusing

8. When he heard about a dentist who could cure toothaches by telegraph, the general said, "It's nothing but humbug!" The word *humbug* means
   Ⓐ remarkable.
   Ⓑ nonsense.
   Ⓒ exciting.
   Ⓓ expensive.

9. "What an abominable memory you have!" the general said angrily. The word *abominable* means
   Ⓐ disgusting or horrible.
   Ⓑ marvelous or wonderful.
   Ⓒ reliable or dependable.
   Ⓓ odd or strange.

10. After the dentist pulled the tooth, General Kurlov's pain eventually subsided. The word *subsided* means
   Ⓐ increased.
   Ⓑ decreased.
   Ⓒ throbbed.
   Ⓓ annoyed.

Answers				
6.	Ⓐ	Ⓑ	Ⓒ	Ⓓ
7.	Ⓐ	Ⓑ	Ⓒ	Ⓓ
8.	Ⓐ	Ⓑ	Ⓒ	Ⓓ
9.	Ⓐ	Ⓑ	Ⓒ	Ⓓ
10.	Ⓐ	Ⓑ	Ⓒ	Ⓓ

How many questions did you answer correctly? Circle your score below. Then fill in your **Comprehension** score on the **Test-Taker Score Chart** on the inside of the back cover.

Number Correct	1	2	3	4	5	6	7	8	9	10
My Score	10	20	30	40	50	60	70	80	90	100

Go on ➤

II. Mechanics (capitalization, punctuation, the comma, spelling, and grammar)

Fill in the circle next to the correct answer.

1. Which sentence has an error in capitalization?
   - Ⓐ The dentist lived in the city of Sarloff in russia.
   - Ⓑ General Kurlov agreed to have his tooth pulled the next day.
   - Ⓒ He asked Ivan, "Is Stallworth the name of the dentist?"
   - Ⓓ We read "A Horsey Name" in our English class on Friday

2. Which sentence has an error in punctuation?
   - Ⓐ Ivan said, "It's a common name, but I can't remember what it is."
   - Ⓑ He rinsed his mouth with lemon juice, vinegar, and a variety of medicines.
   - Ⓒ "I can't stand this any longer!" he cried out in pain.
   - Ⓓ Did the dentist check the generals mouth with great care?

3. Which sentence needs a comma or does not use the comma correctly?
   - Ⓐ Ivan, a servant, offered the general an unusual suggestion.
   - Ⓑ The dentist often went to people's homes but he also helped people by mail.
   - Ⓒ Naturally, everyone tried to think of the dentist's name.
   - Ⓓ Anton Chekhov was born in the town of Taganrog on January 17, 1860.

4. Which sentence has an error in spelling in the underlined word?
   - Ⓐ General Kurlov sought <u>releif</u> from a terrible toothache.
   - Ⓑ Is it <u>possible</u> for a dentist to cure a toothache without seeing the patient?
   - Ⓒ None of the family members <u>guessed</u> the name of the dentist.
   - Ⓓ Ivan did not wish to <u>disappoint</u> the general.

5. Which of the following has a mistake in grammar?
   - Ⓐ The dentist pulled out the aching tooth. Soon the general felt better.
   - Ⓑ All of the remedies were useless.
   - Ⓒ Ivan shook his head sadly.
   - Ⓓ Ivan finally remembered the name. And rushed to the general.

Answers				
1.	Ⓐ	Ⓑ	Ⓒ	Ⓓ
2.	Ⓐ	Ⓑ	Ⓒ	Ⓓ
3.	Ⓐ	Ⓑ	Ⓒ	Ⓓ
4.	Ⓐ	Ⓑ	Ⓒ	Ⓓ
5.	Ⓐ	Ⓑ	Ⓒ	Ⓓ

How many questions did you answer correctly? Circle your score below. Then fill in your **Mechanics** score on the **Test-Taker Score Chart** on the inside of the back cover.

Number Correct	1	2	3	4	5
Your Score	20	40	60	80	100

Go on ➤

III. Writing

Answer the questions that follow. You may look back at the story as often as you wish.

1. Complete the chart below by listing 10 *different* names that were suggested for the dentist in Sarloff. Then explain why each name was suggested. One has been done for you.

Names Suggested for the Dentist in Sarloff	The Reason the Name Was Suggested
1. Colt (or Colton)	A colt is a young male horse.
2.	
3.	
4.	
5.	
6.	
7.	
8.	
9.	
10.	

Go on ➤

2. Suppose that you want to tell someone the story "A Horsey Name." To assist you, first fill in the story map below.

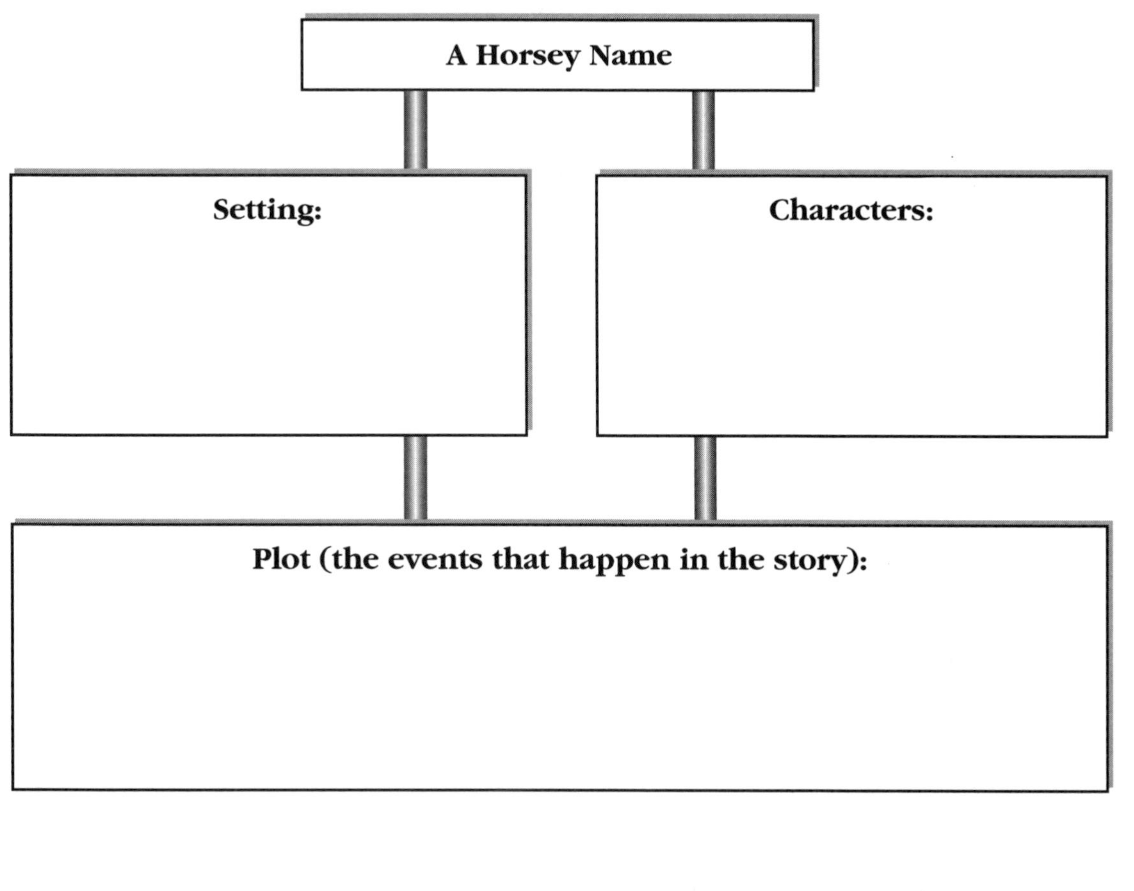

Now summarize "A Horsey Name" by using the information on the story map.

____

____

____

____

____

____

____

____

____

Go on ➤

3. Suppose that Ivan had remembered the dentist's name at the beginning of the story and that General Kurlov *had* sent the dentist a telegram and his fee. How do you think the story would have ended? Pretend that you are General Kurlov and explain what happened.

General Kurlov Speaks

It all started when ______________________________

Go on ➤

4. Read the following expressions:

- **Absence makes the heart grow fonder.**
- **Out of sight, out of mind.**
- **No pain, no gain.**
- **What can't be cured must be endured.**

Circle the two expressions that you believe best relate to the story. Then explain how each expression applies to the story. Use examples and details from the selection to support your answer.

Be sure to check your writing for correct spelling, capitalization, punctuation, and grammar.

Stop

DIRECTIONS
Read the article. Then answer the questions that follow.

The Exodusters

One result of the Civil War (1861–1865) was that slavery was abolished in the United States of America. But in the 1870s, life was still very difficult for many African Americans in the South. To ensure equal treatment for all citizens, United States Federal troops were stationed in the South. The presence of these soldiers, however, angered some white Southerners. They felt as if they were being treated like a vanquished enemy.

By 1877 the last United States soldiers had left the South. Despite this, there was resentment by some Southerners against their African-American neighbors. Acts of violence against African Americans periodically occurred.

Many African Americans felt that a brighter future lay not in the South but in the new territories of the American West. There were also a number of incentives to migrate to the West. The Homestead Act of 1862 granted 160 acres of government land to anyone who settled on that land for five years and established a ranch or a farm. Furthermore, there were numerous job opportunities on the railroads being built across the West and in the new towns that were springing up.

A huge African-American migration led by a former slave and Civil War veteran Henry Adams began in 1879. This migration to the state of Kansas and points farther west was called the Exodus of 1879. Those who migrated called themselves "Exodusters."

In 1879 alone, nearly 40,000 African Americans made their way to Kansas. Some of them came by land, and others traveled by boat up the Mississippi River. They were all seeking the same things: opportunity and freedom.

For additional exercises and a story about other pioneers who made their way to the West, see "The Day the Sun Came Out" in *More Conflicts* in *Goodman's Five-Star Stories,* Level H.

Life was not easy for these new homesteaders. They faced many hardships and challenges, including dust storms, droughts, and even swarms of insects that destroyed their new crops. Some of the Exodusters could not read and write. All of them were very poor, but they worked hard and many managed to prosper.

One of the most notable of the Exodusters was Junius Groves. He migrated to Kansas with less than a dollar in his pocket. At first, Groves and his wife, Matilda, worked for another farmer. Their dream was to save enough money to buy their own farm. Eventually they managed to do that. They started by planting potatoes, onions, and other vegetables on their newly purchased land. Junius Groves was a gifted farmer who developed ingenious methods for cultivating crops. Before long, his land was yielding a much greater harvest than any farm in the area. Groves's reputation grew along with the land he acquired, and he eventually became known as the "Potato King of the World." By 1910 the Groves's farm stretched across 2,100 acres and was considered one of the finest farms in Kansas.

After they arrived in the West, some of the Exodusters decided to build their own towns. One of the best-known of these was Nicodemus, Kansas. By 1880 Nicodemus had 650 residents and a large and bustling business district that included a school, a general store, and a post office. Within just a few years, Nicodemus also had its own newspaper and baseball team.

Many of the Exodusters did not stay in Kansas but went even farther west. Soon they were joined by many more African Americans who were seeking greater freedom and prosperity in the American West. When the Oklahoma territory opened in 1889, there were about 10,000 African Americans among the 50,000 people who settled there. The Exodusters established 27 all-black towns in Oklahoma, much like Nicodemus and the other Exoduster towns in Kansas.

Yet Oklahoma wasn't the only western state to which African Americans migrated. Between 1870 and 1910 the African-American population in the United States doubled, but in the western states of Montana, Idaho, Wyoming, Colorado, New Mexico, Arizona, Utah, and Nevada it increased far more dramatically.

Between 1870 and 1910 more than 60 all-black towns were established in the western United States. Many of them prospered for decades until the Great Depression of the 1930s, when the poor economy of the United States, coupled with a severe drought, proved disastrous. Many residents of those towns were forced to pack up and move elsewhere. Today, these places are mostly "ghost town"—towns filled with empty houses and deserted streets that stand as a reminder of the busy life that once flourished there years ago.

Still, Nicodemus, Kansas, has survived to this day. It is the last remaining town built by the Exodusters—a living monument to the spirit and courage of those thousands of African Americans who headed West long ago to pursue their dream of freedom.

Go on ➤

I. Reading Comprehension Skills

Fill in the circle next to the correct answer.

1. What is the article mostly about?
   Ⓐ the African-American migration to the West after the Civil War
   Ⓑ some of the hardships the homesteaders faced in the West
   Ⓒ Henry Adams, a former Civil War veteran
   Ⓓ Nicodemus, Kansas, a town built by the Exodusters

2. Which group of words belongs in the empty box below?
   Ⓐ did not work hard
   Ⓑ could read and write very well
   Ⓒ were seeking greater job opportunities
   Ⓓ were quite wealthy

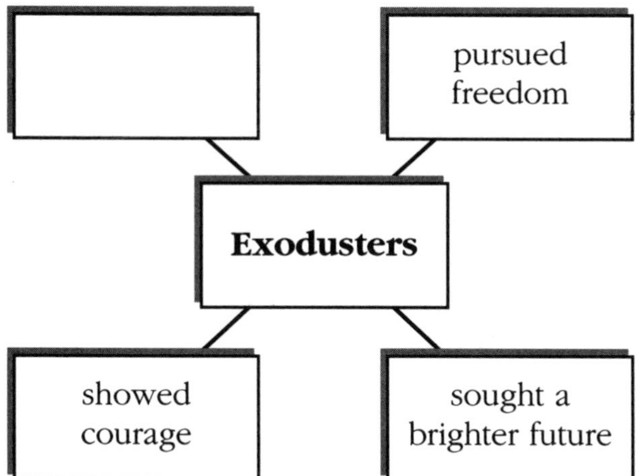

3. We may infer that Junius Groves
   Ⓐ practiced the very same farming methods that had always been used.
   Ⓑ was not willing to make sacrifices to achieve his dream.
   Ⓒ had no influence at all on other farmers in the region.
   Ⓓ eventually became very rich.

4. What was the purpose of the Homestead Act of 1862?
   Ⓐ to provide relief to farmers whose crops had been lost in the drought
   Ⓑ to encourage people to settle in the West
   Ⓒ to offer jobs on the railroads
   Ⓓ to improve the quality of education in the United States

5. According to the article, what happened to the black population in the West between 1870 and 1910?
   Ⓐ It decreased dramatically.
   Ⓑ It increased slightly.
   Ⓒ It increased substantially.
   Ⓓ It remained about the same as in previous years.

Answers				
1.	Ⓐ	Ⓑ	Ⓒ	Ⓓ
2.	Ⓐ	Ⓑ	Ⓒ	Ⓓ
3.	Ⓐ	Ⓑ	Ⓒ	Ⓓ
4.	Ⓐ	Ⓑ	Ⓒ	Ⓓ
5.	Ⓐ	Ⓑ	Ⓒ	Ⓓ

Go on ➤

6. The main cause for the decline of the towns built by the Exodusters was
   Ⓐ reduced tourist trade.
   Ⓑ larger populations than the towns could handle.
   Ⓒ arguments among politicians in the towns.
   Ⓓ poor economic conditions.

7. The article suggests that the Exodusters
   Ⓐ were foolish to have left their homes to journey westward.
   Ⓑ never achieved any success.
   Ⓒ had very few incentives to migrate to the West.
   Ⓓ demonstrated courage and spirit in the pursuit of freedom.

8. Some Southerners were unhappy because they felt as if they were being treated like a vanquished enemy. The word *vanquished* means
   Ⓐ respected.
   Ⓑ defeated.
   Ⓒ silly.
   Ⓓ powerful.

9. Junius Groves was a gifted farmer who developed ingenious methods for cultivating his crops. The word *ingenious* means
   Ⓐ time-honored.
   Ⓑ surprising.
   Ⓒ ridiculous.
   Ⓓ very clever.

10. A severe drought proved disastrous and forced many of the residents to pack up and move. Something that is *disastrous*
   Ⓐ causes much suffering or loss.
   Ⓑ is difficult to figure out.
   Ⓒ can easily be overcome.
   Ⓓ is an occasion for celebration.

Answers				
6.	Ⓐ	Ⓑ	Ⓒ	Ⓓ
7.	Ⓐ	Ⓑ	Ⓒ	Ⓓ
8.	Ⓐ	Ⓑ	Ⓒ	Ⓓ
9.	Ⓐ	Ⓑ	Ⓒ	Ⓓ
10.	Ⓐ	Ⓑ	Ⓒ	Ⓓ

How many questions did you answer correctly? Circle your score below. Then fill in your **Comprehension** score on the **Test-Taker Score Chart** on the inside of the back cover.

Number Correct	1	2	3	4	5	6	7	8	9	10
My Score	10	20	30	40	50	60	70	80	90	100

Go on ➤

II. Mechanics (capitalization, punctuation, the comma, spelling, and grammar)

Fill in the circle next to the correct answer.

1. Which sentence has an error in capitalization?
   - Ⓐ The Homestead Act of 1862 encouraged people to move westward.
   - Ⓑ Many African Americans migrated to the West from the south.
   - Ⓒ Some came by land, and others traveled up the Mississippi River.
   - Ⓓ The Exodusters migrated to Kansas, Arizona, New Mexico, and other states.

2. Which sentence has an error in punctuation?
   - Ⓐ Dr. William C. D. Harris has written an article called "An Exoduster's Story."
   - Ⓑ Don't you think it's extremely difficult to start a new life elsewhere?
   - Ⓒ One of the best-known Exoduster towns was Nicodemus Kansas.
   - Ⓓ Nicodemus had 680 residents by 1880.

3. Which sentence needs a comma or does not use the comma correctly?
   - Ⓐ More jobs were available, but the work was very hard.
   - Ⓑ The Exodusters faced dust storms, droughts, and swarms of insects.
   - Ⓒ However they found ways to deal with the hardships.
   - Ⓓ Many towns prospered for decades and then declined.

4. Which sentence has an error in spelling in the underlined word?
   - Ⓐ According to the article, acts of violence often <u>occured</u>.
   - Ⓑ What was the <u>principal</u> reason that the Exodusters migrated?
   - Ⓒ Settlers were entitled to <u>receive</u> 160 acres of land.
   - Ⓓ Junius Groves and his wife saved enough money to buy <u>their</u> own farm.

5. Which sentence has an error in grammar?
   - Ⓐ Some of the new settlers didn't know nothing about farming.
   - Ⓑ They were hard workers who learned very quickly.
   - Ⓒ They did their best to handle challenges.
   - Ⓓ Many settlers wrote letters to friends.

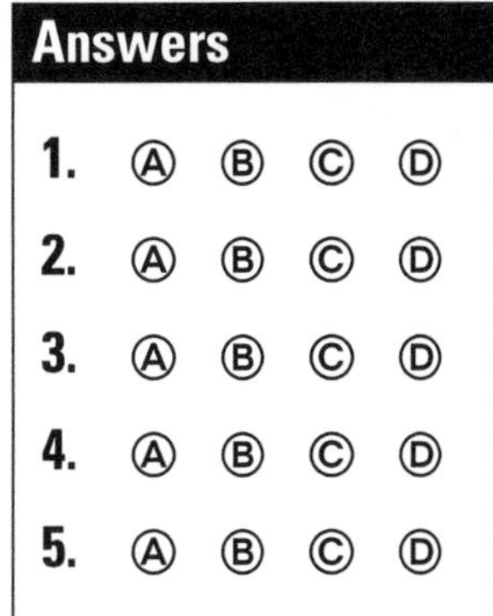

Answers

1.	Ⓐ	Ⓑ	Ⓒ	Ⓓ
2.	Ⓐ	Ⓑ	Ⓒ	Ⓓ
3.	Ⓐ	Ⓑ	Ⓒ	Ⓓ
4.	Ⓐ	Ⓑ	Ⓒ	Ⓓ
5.	Ⓐ	Ⓑ	Ⓒ	Ⓓ

How many questions did you answer correctly? Circle your score below. Then fill in your **Mechanics** score on the **Test-Taker Score Chart** on the inside of the back cover.

Number Correct	1	2	3	4	5
Your Score	20	40	60	80	100

Go on ➤

III. Writing

Answer the questions. You may look back at the article as often as you wish.

1. On the following page, you will write an essay about the Exodusters. First review the article. Then, in the space below, write some important facts and dates from the article.

Go on ➤

2. Now write an essay about the Exodusters. Be sure to explain the following:
   - who the Exodusters were
   - what the Exodusters did and why
   - what challenges the Exodusters faced.

   Use information from your notes to assist you. Organize your essay carefully.

Be sure to check your writing for correct spelling, capitalization, punctuation, and grammar.

The Exodusters

Go on ➤

3. Many people have probably never heard of the Exodusters. Write a letter to a friend telling him or her about Junius Groves and Nicodemus, Kansas.

____
(Date)

____

____
(Your address)

Dear ________________,

____

____

____

____

____

____

____

____

____

____

____

____

Your friend,

____

Go on ➤

4. Write a descriptive essay entitled "Moving Day." Try to capture the hustle and bustle and emotions that are associated with moving. Base your essay on personal experience, or use your imagination to paint a picture. Use vivid verbs and powerful adjectives to portray the sights, sounds, and feelings that accompany moving.

Be sure to check your writing for correct spelling, capitalization, punctuation, and grammar.

Moving Day

Go on ➤

IV. Study Skills

Interpreting a Table. Study the table. Then answer the questions that follow.

Some Important Battles of the Civil War

Battle	State	Date	Commanders		Casualties*		Results
			North	South	North	South	
Fort Donelson	Tennessee	February 1862	Grant	Buckner	2,800	16,500	Many historians consider this the North's first important victory.
Second Battle of Bull Run	Virginia	August 1862	Pope	Lee	14,500	9,200	The North was badly defeated. The South regained almost all of Virginia.
Antietam	Maryland	September 1862	McClellan	Lee	12,000	12,700	This was the bloodiest day of the Civil War. There was no clear victory for either side, but Lee retreated to Virginia.
Fredericksburg	Virginia	December 1862	Burnside	Lee	12,700	5,300	This was a severe defeat for the North.
Chancellorsville	Virginia	May 1863	Hooker	Lee	17,300	12,750	This was a great victory for Lee and the South, but Stonewall Jackson, an important southern military leader, was killed.
Vicksburg Campaign	Mississippi	May to July 1863	Grant/	Pemberton	8,000	39,000	The North gained control of the last major southern port on the Mississippi River. The North now had control of the entire Mississippi River.
Gettysburg	Pennsylvania	July 1863	Meade	Lee	23,000	25,500	Most historians consider this Northern victory the turning point in the war.

*Casualties are approximate and include soldiers killed, wounded, captured, and missing.

Go on ➤

1. Where and when was the Battle of Antietam fought?

____

2. What were the names of the generals of the Northern and Southern armies in the Battle of Fredericksburg?

____

3. What were the casualties to each side in the Second Battle of Bull Run?

____

4. Why is the Battle of Gettysburg considered so important?

____

5. Although the South defeated the North in the Battle of Chancellorsville, the victory to the South was not completely satisfactory. Why?

____

6. What battle do many historians consider the North's first important victory?

____

7. What battle was fought in December 1862?

____

8. In what battle did General Robert E. Lee oppose General George C. Meade?

____

9. What battle was fought in the state of Tennessee?

____

10. Why was victory in the Vicksburg Campaign so important to the North?

____

Stop

DIRECTIONS
Read the story. Then answer the questions that follow.

The Revolt of Mother

excerpt based on a story by Mary E. Wilkins Freeman

Mary E. Wilkins Freeman (1852–1930) is the author of more than 225 short stories, 12 novels, and a play. She is noted for her realistic portraits of New England life. Her best-known character is probably Sarah Penn, a strong-willed and determined woman who spoke her mind firmly at a time when it was not fashionable for women to do so.

In this selection from the story "The Revolt of Mother," Sarah has learned that her husband, Adoniram, a wealthy farmer, is planning to build yet another barn on their land.

Sarah Penn was making mince pies. Her husband, Adoniram Penn, liked them better than any other kind. She hurried this morning, since it had been later than usual when she began, and she wanted to have pie baked for dinner. However deep an anger or resentment she might be forced to hold against her husband, she would never fail to attend to his needs. So she made the pies carefully, while across the table she could see, when she glanced out the window, the sight that rankled and pained her patient and steadfast soul—the digging of the cellar for the new barn in the place where Adoniram 40 years ago had promised her their new house should stand.

Adoniram and Sammy, their son, returned for lunch a few minutes after noon. They ate promptly and then rose up and went about their work. Sammy went back to school, while Adoniram went

---

For additional exercises and the complete version of this story, see "'The Revolt of Mother" in *Conflicts* in *Goodman's Five-Star Stories,* Level H.

to work in the yard unloading wood from the wagon. Sarah put away the dishes, while their daughter, Nanny, left to go to the store.

When Nanny was gone, Mrs. Penn went to the door. "Adoniram!" she called.

"Well, what is it?" he replied.

"I just want to see you for a minute."

"I can't leave this wood nohow. I've got to get it unloaded and go for a load of gravel before two o'clock."

"I want to see you just a minute."

"I tell you I can't stop nohow now."

"Adoniram, you come here." Sarah Penn stood in the doorway like a queen. She held her head high, as though it carried a crown; there was in her that patience which made authority royal in her voice. Adoniram went.

Mrs. Penn led the way into the kitchen and pointed to a chair. "Sit down," she said. "I've got something I want to say to you."

He sat down heavily. His face was quite hard and showed no emotion, but he looked at her with uneasy eyes, "Well, what is it?" he asked.

"I want to know what you're buildin' that new barn for."

"I ain't got nothing to say about it."

"It can't be you think you need another barn?"

"I tell you I ain't got nothing to say about it, and I ain't goin' to say nothin'."

"Are you going to buy more cows?"

Adoniram did not reply; he shut his mouth tight.

"I know you are. Now, look here," said Sarah Penn, "I'm goin' to talk real plain to you; I never have since I married you, but I'm goin' to now. I ain't never complained, and I ain't goin' to complain now, but I'm goin' to talk plain. You see this room here. You look at it well. You see there ain't no carpet on the floor, and you see the wallpaper is all dirty and droppin' off the walls. We ain't had no new paper on it for ten years, and then I put it on myself, and it didn't cost but pennies a roll.

"You see this room, Adoniram. It's all the one I've had to work in and sit in since we were married. It's all the room our daughter Nanny's got for company, and all her friends have better than this, and their fathers don't have half the means that you have. It's the room she'll have to be married in! We were married in my mother's parlor, with a carpet on the floor, and stuffed furniture, and a mahogany table. And this is all the room my daughter will have to be married in! Look here, Adoniram!"

Sarah Penn marched across the room. She flung open a door and disclosed a tiny bedroom, only large enough for a bed and a dresser.

"There, Adoniram," she said, "there's all the room I've had to sleep in for forty years. All my children were born there—the two that died, and the two that's livin'. I was sick with a fever there."

She threw open another door. A narrow, crooked flight of stairs wound upward from it. "There, Adoniram," she said, "I want you to look at those two unfinished rooms that are all the places our son and daughter have had to sleep in all their lives. Those are the places they have to sleep in. They ain't as good as your horse's stall. They ain't as warm and tight."

Sarah Penn went back and stood in front of her husband. "Now," she said, "I want to know if you think you're doin' right accordin' to what you said. Here, when we were married forty years ago, you promised me faithful that we should have a new house built in that lot over in the field before the year was out. You said you had money enough, and you wouldn't ask me to live in no such place as this. It is forty years now, and you've been makin' more money, and I've been savin' of it, and you ain't built no house yet. You've built sheds and cow-houses and one new barn. And now you're goin' to build another. I want to know if you think it's right. You're lodgin' your dumb beasts better than you are your own flesh and blood. I want to know if you think it's right."

"I ain't got nothin' to say."

"You can't say nothin' without ownin' it ain't right, Adoniram."

Mrs. Penn's face was burning; her eyes gleamed. She had pleaded her case very eloquently. But Adoniram remained silent.

"Adoniram, ain't you got nothin' to say?" said Mrs. Penn.

"I've got to get that load of gravel. I can't stand here talkin' all day."

"Adoniram, won't you think it over, and have a house built there instead of a barn?"

But Adoniram kept to his obstinate, stubborn silence.

"I ain't got nothin' to say."

Go on ➤

I. Reading Comprehension Skills

Fill in the circle next to the correct answer.

1. This story tells mostly about
   Ⓐ family life in a New England town.
   Ⓑ how a woman decides to speak up for what she thinks is right.
   Ⓒ why it is necessary for a farmer to build a barn.
   Ⓓ how work on a farm is never really finished.

2. What was Sarah Penn's major complaint?
   Ⓐ Her husband worked so hard that he was endangering his health.
   Ⓑ Their house did not have a carpet, and the wallpaper was peeling.
   Ⓒ Adoniram was building a new barn instead of a new house.
   Ⓓ Their children's rooms were not finished yet.

3. Which statement suggests that Adoniram was not poor?
   Ⓐ He and his wife slept in a tiny room just large enough to hold a dresser and a bed.
   Ⓑ Their children's rooms were not as warm and tight as his horse's stall.
   Ⓒ Nanny's friends had better rooms, and their fathers didn't have half the means that Adoniram had.
   Ⓓ Adoniram and Sarah were married in a room with a carpet on the floor and fine furniture.

4. Which statement correctly describes Sarah Penn?
   Ⓐ She decided it was time to "talk plain" to Adoniram.
   Ⓑ She was so angry with her husband that she began to neglect him.
   Ⓒ She often bitterly complained to Adoniram.
   Ⓓ She was sorry that she had married Adoniram.

5. It is likely that Adoniram did not respond to his wife's questions because
   Ⓐ he did not understand what she meant.
   Ⓑ he had already discussed the situation with her that morning.
   Ⓒ he was angry with Sarah for shirking her tasks on the farm.
   Ⓓ he was embarrassed and could not provide appropriate answers.

Answers				
1.	Ⓐ	Ⓑ	Ⓒ	Ⓓ
2.	Ⓐ	Ⓑ	Ⓒ	Ⓓ
3.	Ⓐ	Ⓑ	Ⓒ	Ⓓ
4.	Ⓐ	Ⓑ	Ⓒ	Ⓓ
5.	Ⓐ	Ⓑ	Ⓒ	Ⓓ

Go on ➤

6. We may infer that the author
   Ⓐ feels sorry for Adoniram.
   Ⓑ sympathizes with Sarah.
   Ⓒ has never worked on a farm.
   Ⓓ does not know much about human nature.

7. What is the tone of the story?
   Ⓐ humorous
   Ⓑ mysterious
   Ⓒ serious
   Ⓓ terrifying

8. When Sarah saw the cellar of the new barn, the sight of it rankled her. The word *rankled* means
   Ⓐ frightened or shocked.
   Ⓑ amused.
   Ⓒ irritated or caused pain.
   Ⓓ thrilled.

9. She pleaded her case eloquently, but Adoniram remained silent. When you express yourself *eloquently*, you
   Ⓐ speak with force and grace.
   Ⓑ do not communicate well.
   Ⓒ are not certain of your facts.
   Ⓓ shout as loudly as you can.

10. At the end of the story, Adoniram was obstinate and refused to answer Sarah. The word *obstinate* means
   Ⓐ confused.
   Ⓑ furious.
   Ⓒ stubborn.
   Ⓓ tired.

Answers				
6.	Ⓐ	Ⓑ	Ⓒ	Ⓓ
7.	Ⓐ	Ⓑ	Ⓒ	Ⓓ
8.	Ⓐ	Ⓑ	Ⓒ	Ⓓ
9.	Ⓐ	Ⓑ	Ⓒ	Ⓓ
10.	Ⓐ	Ⓑ	Ⓒ	Ⓓ

How many questions did you answer correctly? Circle your score below. Then fill in your **Comprehension** score on the **Test-Taker Score Chart** on the inside of the back cover.

Number Correct	1	2	3	4	5	6	7	8	9	10
My Score	10	20	30	40	50	60	70	80	90	100

Go on ➤

II. Mechanics (capitalization, punctuation, the comma, spelling, and grammar)

Fill in the circle next to the correct answer.

1. Which sentence has an error in capitalization?
   - Ⓐ Mary E. Wilkins Freeman was born in Massachusetts on March 13, 1825.
   - Ⓑ "The Revolt of Mother" is Freeman's most famous short story.
   - Ⓒ Sarah Penn asked, "do you think what you're doing is right?"
   - Ⓓ Adoniram planned to build another barn on his property in New England.

2. Which sentence is not punctuated correctly?
   - Ⓐ Mr and Mrs Penn had been married for 40 years.
   - Ⓑ She suddenly exclaimed, "I have something to tell you!"
   - Ⓒ Their children's room wasn't as warm as his horse's stall.
   - Ⓓ Although Sarah pleaded her case with much passion, Adoniram refused to answer.

3. Which sentence needs a comma or does not use the comma correctly?
   - Ⓐ Adoniram, a wealthy farmer, lived in a relatively modest house.
   - Ⓑ Sarah finished making the pie and bread was baking in the oven.
   - Ⓒ Adoniram had built sheds, cow-houses, fences, and a new barn.
   - Ⓓ However, he was a man who could be described as strong and silent.

4. Which sentence has an error in spelling in the underlined word?
   - Ⓐ Adoniram was <u>extremely</u> careful about how he spent his money.
   - Ⓑ Sarah hoped that <u>eventually</u> he would keep his promise.
   - Ⓒ He claimed that he had to attend to other <u>busness</u>.
   - Ⓓ Freeman has <u>written</u> short stories, novels, and a play.

5. Which sentence has an error in grammar?
   - Ⓐ Good manners are important in dealing with people.
   - Ⓑ Earlier, Adoniram drove to town.
   - Ⓒ He began to leave, but Sarah called him back.
   - Ⓓ Adoniram and Sarah was both thrifty people.

Answers				
1.	Ⓐ	Ⓑ	Ⓒ	Ⓓ
2.	Ⓐ	Ⓑ	Ⓒ	Ⓓ
3.	Ⓐ	Ⓑ	Ⓒ	Ⓓ
4.	Ⓐ	Ⓑ	Ⓒ	Ⓓ
5.	Ⓐ	Ⓑ	Ⓒ	Ⓓ

How many questions did you answer correctly? Circle your score below. Then fill in your **Mechanics** score on the **Test-Taker Score Chart** on the inside of the back cover.

Number Correct	1	2	3	4	5
Your Score	20	40	60	80	100

Go on ➤

III. Writing

Answer the questions that follow. You may look back at the story as often as you wish.

1. Complete the charts below by filling in three character traits for Sarah Penn and three character traits for Adoniram Penn. Then provide words or phrases that describe each character trait. Refer to the selection to identify clearly the character traits and supporting information.

Sarah Penn

Character Trait	Supporting Information

Adoniram Penn

Character Trait	Supporting Information

Go on ➤

2. Sarah Penn was angry because her husband, Adoniram, was planning to build a new barn. Why was Sarah so opposed to the barn? On the chart below, list some reasons.

Reasons Why Sarah Was Opposed to the New Barn

3. Why do you think Adoniram decided to build another barn instead of a house? Do you agree with his decision? Explain.

Go on ➤

4. Read the following statement:

   Adoniram Penn neglected his family.

   Do you agree or disagree with this statement? Give several reasons to support your position.

   I think that Adoniram Penn ____

   ____

   ____

   ____

   ____

   ____

   ____

   ____

   ____

   ____

5. Sarah Penn has been called a "woman who was far ahead of her time." Why do you think she has been described this way? Remember that the story was written more than 100 years ago.

   ____

   ____

   ____

   ____

   ____

   ____

   ____

   ____

   ____

Go on ➤

6. Sarah Penn demanded to know if her husband thought that what he was doing was right, but Adoniram refused to discuss the situation.

   Write an essay about an argument, disagreement, or dispute that was (or was not) settled to everyone's satisfaction. Tell who was involved, what the main issue was, and whether or not the problem was finally resolved.

Be sure to check your writing for correct spelling, capitalization, punctuation, and grammar.

A Dispute

Stop

DIRECTIONS
Read the article. Then answer the questions that follow.

An Amazing Discovery

On the morning of July 24, 1911, dawn broke rainy and cool high in the Andes Mountains of Peru. Hiram Bingham, a 36-year-old American explorer born in Hawaii, stood on a tall ridge in a thick forest and paused to gaze around. Low clouds obscured the tops of the mountains.

Hiram Bingham was on a mission. He had traveled to this place—the most inaccessible region of Peru—because he suspected that a great discovery might be made here. He had heard of a place deep in these Peruvian forests that contained large stone ruins. Bingham suspected that these ruins were of momentous historical importance. He suspected that they were the remains of Machu Picchu, the fabled "lost city" of the Incan Empire.

In the 14th and 15th centuries, the Incas, a Native American people of South America, established the largest, wealthiest, and most powerful empire in the Western Hemisphere. It stretched for more than 2,500 miles and took in parts of what is today Peru, Chile, Columbia, Ecuador, Bolivia, and Argentina. It is not possible to determine the exact population, but as many as 16 million people may have inhabited this huge region, all of them subjects of the vast Incan Empire.

The Incan Empire had created some of the most impressive architecture of its time. Among the achievements were massive stone

---

For additional exercises and a story with a related setting and theme, see "The Country of the Blind" in *More Conflicts* in *Goodman's Five-Star Stories,* Level H.

palaces, fortresses, and the huge Temple of the Sun in the capital city of Cuzco. Though many of these great buildings have endured to this day, the Incan civilization itself is long gone. The empire was invaded and defeated by Spanish soldiers led by Francisco Pizarro in 1552.

Pizarro appointed Manco Capac to assume the Incan throne. Several years later, Manco led a revolt against the Spanish. He was defeated and fled into the Peruvian mountains with an enormous treasure of silver and gold. There he established a new capital city, where he ruled for 35 years. With the passing of time, no one knew precisely where that capital city had been—but Hiram Bingham thought that he might discover it in Machu Picchu.

Led by a native guide named Melchor Arteaga, Bingham and his two assistants made their way up and down the steep, winding trails that led through the mountains. It was not an easy trip. As they walked along, they warily watched for poisonous snakes. They once had to crawl across a primitive bridge made of logs that had been tied together. Below the ancient bridge was a dangerous, rushing river. Finally, sometime in the midafternoon, Arteaga told Bingham that the ruins he was seeking lay just over the next hill.

His heart pounding with excitement, Bingham scrambled up to the top of the hill and looked at the peaceful valley below. At first, he saw only a very thick tangle of trees. As he looked more closely, Bingham detected a number of stone walls to his left. Then he noticed several stone houses, arranged around what must have been a central plaza at one time.

Bingham made his way to the top of the next ridge and looked down. He saw a tremendous stone building; it seemed to be a temple of some kind. Bingham suspected that it had been used for Incan religious ceremonies. Near the temple was a stone stairway, and at the bottom step was a stone basin with small channels that obviously had once carried water.

Bingham also noticed an intricately carved stone column about 20 inches high. He immediately knew what it was—a sundial—a very important instrument used in ceremonies by the sun-worshipping Incas. Still breathless with excitement, Bingham took a moment to jot down a few words in his notebook: "Fine ruins. Houses, streets, stairs. Finely cut stone."

Hiram Bingham had indeed found Machu Picchu, the "lost city" of the Incas. Of course, Bingham did not really "discover" Machu Picchu any more than Columbus really "discovered" America. Native people were already living in both places. But like Columbus,

Bingham brought news of what he had found to the attention of the world. Moreover, finding Machu Picchu was one of the most important archaeological discoveries of the 20th century.

Today, Machu Picchu is the chief tourist attraction in Peru. As for Hiram Bingham—he went on to achieve further success in his life. He was an army commander during World War I, and from 1925 to 1933 he served as a United States senator for the state of Connecticut. Despite his various careers, Hiram Bingham thought of himself as an explorer, and he considered his discovery of Machu Picchu to be his greatest achievement.

In 1948 the road to Machu Picchu was named the Hiram Bingham Highway in Bingham's honor.

Go on ➤

I. Reading Comprehension Skills

Fill in the circle next to the correct answer.

1. What is the article mostly about?
   Ⓐ how Hiram Bingham became an explorer
   Ⓑ some impressive achievements of the Incan Empire
   Ⓒ architecture in South America in the 14th and 15th centuries
   Ⓓ Bingham's discovery of the ruins of Machu Picchu

2. Which sentence is *not* true of the Incan Empire?
   Ⓐ It was once the most powerful empire in the Western Hemisphere.
   Ⓑ It stretched for more than 2,500 miles.
   Ⓒ None of the buildings of the empire are still standing today.
   Ⓓ The empire was invaded by Spanish soldiers in 1552.

3. It probably took a long time to find the ruins of Machu Picchu because
   Ⓐ they were located in a place that was very difficult and dangerous to reach.
   Ⓑ armed guards kept people away from the region.
   Ⓒ it was not possible to cross the bridge that led to the ruins.
   Ⓓ nobody believed that Machu Picchu once existed.

4. It is believed that the Incan ruler Manco Capac
   Ⓐ succeeded in defeating the Spanish invaders.
   Ⓑ was killed by Francisco Pizarro.
   Ⓒ fled into the mountains of Peru with much silver and gold.
   Ⓓ escaped to Bolivia where he lived a life of luxury.

5. It is likely that Bingham realized that his mission was a success when he
   Ⓐ made his way along the steep, winding paths.
   Ⓑ saw what appeared to be a temple with a sundial nearby.
   Ⓒ noticed a thick tangle of trees in a peaceful valley.
   Ⓓ did not see any poisonous snakes along the way.

Answers

1.	Ⓐ	Ⓑ	Ⓒ	Ⓓ
2.	Ⓐ	Ⓑ	Ⓒ	Ⓓ
3.	Ⓐ	Ⓑ	Ⓒ	Ⓓ
4.	Ⓐ	Ⓑ	Ⓒ	Ⓓ
5.	Ⓐ	Ⓑ	Ⓒ	Ⓓ

Go on ➤

6. According to the article, it is not completely accurate to say that Bingham "discovered" Machu Picchu because
   Ⓐ his two assistants arrived there a few minutes before he did.
   Ⓑ other American explorers had already found the ruins.
   Ⓒ native people were already aware of its existence.
   Ⓓ he failed to make the world aware of the results of his expedition.

7. What is the main purpose of the article?
   Ⓐ to provide information
   Ⓑ to make the reader smile
   Ⓒ to change the reader's mind
   Ⓓ to make the reader feel sad

8. Low clouds obscured the tops of the mountains. The word *obscured* means
   Ⓐ hid from view.
   Ⓑ drifted by.
   Ⓒ reflected.
   Ⓓ caused rain.

9. The ruins were located in the most inaccessible region of Peru. The word *inaccessible* means
   Ⓐ the highest point.
   Ⓑ hard to reach.
   Ⓒ perilous.
   Ⓓ untamed or wild.

10. Bingham suspected that the ruins were of momentous historical importance. The word *momentous* means
   Ⓐ possible.
   Ⓑ fairly useful.
   Ⓒ not too important.
   Ⓓ extremely important.

Answers				
6.	Ⓐ	Ⓑ	Ⓒ	Ⓓ
7.	Ⓐ	Ⓑ	Ⓒ	Ⓓ
8.	Ⓐ	Ⓑ	Ⓒ	Ⓓ
9.	Ⓐ	Ⓑ	Ⓒ	Ⓓ
10.	Ⓐ	Ⓑ	Ⓒ	Ⓓ

How many questions did you answer correctly? Circle your score below. Then fill in your **Comprehension** score on the **Test-Taker Score Chart** on the inside of the back cover.

Number Correct	1	2	3	4	5	6	7	8	9	10
My Score	10	20	30	40	50	60	70	80	90	100

Go on ➤

II. Mechanics (capitalization, punctuation, the comma, spelling, and grammar)

Fill in the circle next to the correct answer.

1. Which sentence has an error in capitalization?
   Ⓐ Hiram Bingham was an American explorer who was born in Hawaii.
   Ⓑ He found the ruins of Machu Picchu on july 24, 1911.
   Ⓒ They were defeated by Spanish soldiers led by Francisco Pizarro.
   Ⓓ Bingham was an army commander during World War I.

2. Which sentence is not punctuated correctly?
   Ⓐ The Incan Empire consisted of parts of Peru, Chile, Columbia, Ecuador, and other countries.
   Ⓑ The huge Temple of the Sun, for example, was one of the empire's most impressive buildings.
   Ⓒ Bingham's heart was pounding, and he couldn't believe his eyes.
   Ⓓ Hiram Bingham of course was not the first person to gaze upon the remains of Machu Picchu.

3. Which sentence needs a comma or does not use the comma correctly?
   Ⓐ My friend, James Lee, visited Machu Picchu with his family.
   Ⓑ Have you ever been to Machu Picchu Martina?
   Ⓒ No, but I have seen many pictures of the ruins of the city.
   Ⓓ Although Bingham served as a senator for Connecticut, his proudest moments may have occurred when he was an explorer.

4. Which sentence has an error in spelling in the underlined word?
   Ⓐ Bingham jotted down a brief <u>description</u> of Machu Picchu.
   Ⓑ Studies of ancient civilizations <u>yield</u> fascinating information.
   Ⓒ Manco Capac fled with the treasure he had <u>siezed</u>.
   Ⓓ He was in Congress for <u>eight</u> years.

5. Which sentence has an error in grammar?
   Ⓐ It was a dangerous mission, but it turned out very good.
   Ⓑ Bingham and his guide worked together very well.
   Ⓒ The first three lines provide the setting for the article.
   Ⓓ Many professors have visited Machu Picchu.

Answers				
1.	Ⓐ	Ⓑ	Ⓒ	Ⓓ
2.	Ⓐ	Ⓑ	Ⓒ	Ⓓ
3.	Ⓐ	Ⓑ	Ⓒ	Ⓓ
4.	Ⓐ	Ⓑ	Ⓒ	Ⓓ
5.	Ⓐ	Ⓑ	Ⓒ	Ⓓ

How many questions did you answer correctly? Circle your score below. Then fill in your **Mechanics** score on the **Test-Taker Score Chart** on the inside of the back cover.

Number Correct	1	2	3	4	5
Your Score	20	40	60	80	100

Go on ➤

III. Writing

Answer the questions. You may look back at the article as often as you wish.

1. A news story generally answers the questions *who, what, when, where, why,* and *how*. On the lines below, write a news story that tells about Hiram Bingham's discovery of Machu Picchu. Include as many facts from the article as you can. When you have finished your article, be sure to write the headline.

Go on ➤

2. Write an essay about the most interesting place you have ever been to. Provide as many details as you can. Be sure to include the following:

   - the location
   - when you were there
   - what made the place so interesting

   If you prefer, write about a place that you would *like* to visit. Provide details and offer reasons for your selection.

   Be sure to check your writing for correct spelling, capitalization, punctuation, and grammar.

A Fascinating Place

Go on ➤

3. Hiram Bingham had to overcome serious obstacles to find the ruins of Machu Picchu. Write an essay about obstacles you overcame to achieve a goal. Be sure to describe the obstacles involved and explain in detail how you overcame them.

   If you prefer, write about obstacles you are presently encountering, and tell how you plan to, or are working to, overcome them to achieve a goal.

Make sure your essay has an introduction, a body, and a conclusion. Be sure to check your writing for correct spelling, capitalization, punctuation, and grammar.

Overcoming Obstacles

Go on ➤

Stop

DIRECTIONS
Read the biographical sketch of Manuela Williams Crosno and the two poems that follow. Then answer the questions.

Scenes from New Mexico

by Manuela Williams Crosno

Manuela Williams Crosno was born in 1905. She spent most of her life in New Mexico—the state she loved and used as the setting for much of her work. In fact, all of Crosno's stories take place in and around Santa Fe, Taos, and Albuquerque.

Crosno taught English for 17 years at various junior high schools. Her moving article, "Why I Teach School," won first prize in a statewide essay contest.

Crosno's stories have appeared in *New Mexico Magazine*, *New Mexico Quarterly*, and many anthologies. In addition to writing prose, Crosno was a gifted poet and a member of the New Mexico State Poetry Society. A number of her poems are collected in *The Other Side of Nowhere.*

A talented photographer, painter, and illustrator, Crosno also designed and created several large tapestries to accompany a series of stories.

Crosno earned her B.S. and M.S. degrees at New Mexico State University, where her husband, Dr. Donald Crosno, became a professor of Electrical Engineering. The Crosnos were devoted companions who shared, among many other things, their love of literature, nature, art, and their children and grandchildren. In 1983 it was confirmed that Dr. Crosno was suffering from Alzheimer's disease. Four years later he was stricken with pneumonia and died. The couple had been married for 53 years.

For additional exercise and a story by Manuela William Crosno, see "Martinez' Treasure" in *Conflicts* in *Goodman's Five-Star Stories,* Level H.

In the preface to *The Other Side of Nowhere*, Crosno movingly describes her emotions and experiences as a caregiver to her beloved husband. She wrote: "This book . . . is dedicated to those caregivers who are walking or have walked 'the other side' with me. I hope the poems will be a source of tranquility when your world seems to be closing in, a place to which you may retreat and find 'forgotten treasures'—all the memories of those feelings which can *never* really be forgotten."

The two poems that follow are from *The Other Side of Nowhere*. In the first poem, "New Mexico Nocturne," Crosno describes a view she saw from a mountain rim in 1934—the year the couple was married. The mountain was near the couple's home in the Sandia Mountains east of Albuquerque, New Mexico.

In the second poem, "Autumn Dusk," Crosno recalls fond and touching memories of her husband.

Manuela Williams Crosno died at the age of 91 at her home in Las Cruces, New Mexico.

New Mexico Nocturne

Night over the mountains,
 and the world is stilled.

Somewhere down the white and winding road
 a fox slips silently along,
 and in the aspen[1] grove
 silverly the leaves quake in the softened breeze.

A twig breaks in the shadows where the timid deer
 runs swiftly, nostrils distended,[2]
 frightened by this strange scent the winds have found.

Night over the mountains,
and the world is hushed.

Stars are here above the fingertips,
 but to be touched, and out beyond,
 the sleeping valley waits.

Hour before the dawn! The slumbrous mountains now
 raise high their heads and shoulders through the
 dusk, and from some small peak far below
 a mourning dove flies wingward to the sun.

1. **aspen:** A tree whose leaves flutter in the slightest breeze.
2. **distended:** swollen or expanded.

Autumn Dusk

It is autumn at dusk, time for tea;
the table is here before me, set for two,
with candles lighted.

Outside, the sky is a blaze of rose
with deep blue where the dark comes.

It is very quiet in autumn, at dusk.

I close my eyes and there you are
sitting opposite in the armchair,
looking at your long fingers,
speaking intently—looking at me.

My eyes sparkle at your wisdom
and you tell me they are bright,
bright as my crystal earrings.

Watching you, I know, *you are for me,*
a symphony of perfection
I must keep always.

I open my eyes to find only the chair
and the candles across from me.

It is very quiet in the autumn—at dusk.

Go on ➤

I. Reading Comprehension Skills

Fill in the circle next to the correct answer.

1. During what time is "New Mexico Nocturne" set?
   - Ⓐ The entire poem is set during the day.
   - Ⓑ The entire poem is set at night.
   - Ⓒ The poem is set an hour before dawn.
   - Ⓓ The poem begins at night and ends an hour before dawn.

2. In "New Mexico Nocturne" why is the deer frightened?
   - Ⓐ It smells something unusual.
   - Ⓑ It sees a wolf running nearby.
   - Ⓒ It is afraid of the darkness.
   - Ⓓ It has heard a loud shot.

3. In "New Mexico Nocturne" the fact that the "mountains now raise high their heads and shoulders through the dusk" suggests that
   - Ⓐ the mountains are not very tall.
   - Ⓑ animals are moving along the tops of the mountains.
   - Ⓒ daylight is beginning to appear.
   - Ⓓ people are climbing up the mountain.

4. In "Autumn Dusk" we may infer that when the speaker closes her eyes, she sees
   - Ⓐ nothing but darkness.
   - Ⓑ someone she loved dearly.
   - Ⓒ light from the candles.
   - Ⓓ a sky of deep blue.

5. In "Autumn Dusk" when the speaker opens her eyes, she sees
   - Ⓐ her husband sitting across from her.
   - Ⓑ two friends.
   - Ⓒ sparkling crystal earrings.
   - Ⓓ the chair and the candles.

6. In "Autumn Dusk" the speaker probably set two places at the table because
   - Ⓐ she and her husband often had tea together at dusk.
   - Ⓑ she was expecting a guest in five minutes.
   - Ⓒ a friend happened to stop by.
   - Ⓓ she was so upset that she no longer knew what she was doing.

Answers

1. Ⓐ Ⓑ Ⓒ Ⓓ
2. Ⓐ Ⓑ Ⓒ Ⓓ
3. Ⓐ Ⓑ Ⓒ Ⓓ
4. Ⓐ Ⓑ Ⓒ Ⓓ
5. Ⓐ Ⓑ Ⓒ Ⓓ
6. Ⓐ Ⓑ Ⓒ Ⓓ

Go on ➤

7. In "Autumn Dusk" the speaker appears to be
   Ⓐ quite cheerful.
   Ⓑ lonely.
   Ⓒ busy.
   Ⓓ very fearful.

8. Dr. Crosno was stricken with pneumonia and died. The word *stricken* means
   Ⓐ helped.
   Ⓑ recovered.
   Ⓒ treated for.
   Ⓓ struck down.

9. In the preface to *The Other Side of Nowhere,* Crosno addressed her words to the reader. A *preface* is
   Ⓐ an introduction to a book.
   Ⓑ a table of contents.
   Ⓒ a series of illustrations.
   Ⓓ the conclusion to a book.

10. She hoped that her words would be a source of tranquility at a difficult time. The word *tranquility* means
   Ⓐ action.
   Ⓑ peace.
   Ⓒ amazement.
   Ⓓ wealth.

Answers

7. Ⓐ Ⓑ Ⓒ Ⓓ
8. Ⓐ Ⓑ Ⓒ Ⓓ
9. Ⓐ Ⓑ Ⓒ Ⓓ
10. Ⓐ Ⓑ Ⓒ Ⓓ

How many questions did you answer correctly? Circle your score below. Then fill in your **Comprehension** score on the **Test-Taker Score Chart** on the inside of the back cover.

Number Correct	1	2	3	4	5	6	7	8	9	10
My Score	10	20	30	40	50	60	70	80	90	100

Go on ➤

II. Mechanics (capitalization, punctuation, the comma, spelling, and grammar)

Fill in the circle next to the correct answer.

1. Which sentence has an error in capitalization?
   - Ⓐ Manuela Williams Crosno taught English at several junior high schools.
   - Ⓑ These poems are from *The Other Side of Nowhere.*
   - Ⓒ She and her husband had a home not far from the Sandia Mountains east of Albuquerque.
   - Ⓓ Later, they lived for many years in Las Cruces, new Mexico.

2. Which sentence is *not* punctuated correctly?
   - Ⓐ Dr and Mrs Crosno were married for 53 years.
   - Ⓑ Mrs. Crosno's life changed greatly because of her husband's illness.
   - Ⓒ Her poems aren't long, but they're quite moving.
   - Ⓓ Have you ever visited Santa Fe, Taos, or Albuquerque?

3. Which sentence needs a comma or does not use the comma correctly?
   - Ⓐ I met Manuela Williams Crosno, a retired teacher, many years ago.
   - Ⓑ Since I had taught English for a long time, we had a great deal in common.
   - Ⓒ On February 8, 1989 she sent me some poems.
   - Ⓓ I called and said, "Your poetry touched me very deeply."

4. Which sentence has an error in spelling in the underlined word?
   - Ⓐ Have you ever had the <u>occassion</u> to visit the Southwest?
   - Ⓑ After her husband died, Mrs. Crosno was filled with <u>grief</u>.
   - Ⓒ Their <u>marriage</u> lasted for 53 years.
   - Ⓓ Manuela Williams Crosno was <u>truly</u> a remarkable person.

5. Which sentence has an error in grammar?
   - Ⓐ The two poems are quite short.
   - Ⓑ She writes very beautifully.
   - Ⓒ A biography tells about someone's life.
   - Ⓓ Crosno enjoyed reading, writing, painting, and to take walks.

Answers

1. Ⓐ Ⓑ Ⓒ Ⓓ
2. Ⓐ Ⓑ Ⓒ Ⓓ
3. Ⓐ Ⓑ Ⓒ Ⓓ
4. Ⓐ Ⓑ Ⓒ Ⓓ
5. Ⓐ Ⓑ Ⓒ Ⓓ

How many questions did you answer correctly? Circle your score below. Then fill in your **Mechanics** score on the **Test-Taker Score Chart** on the inside of the back cover.

Number Correct	1	2	3	4	5
Your Score	20	40	60	80	100

Go on ➤

III. Writing

Answer the questions. You may look back at the poems as often as you wish.

1. Compare and contrast "New Mexico Nocturne" and "Autumn Dusk." Use the chart below to list how the poems are alike and how they are different.

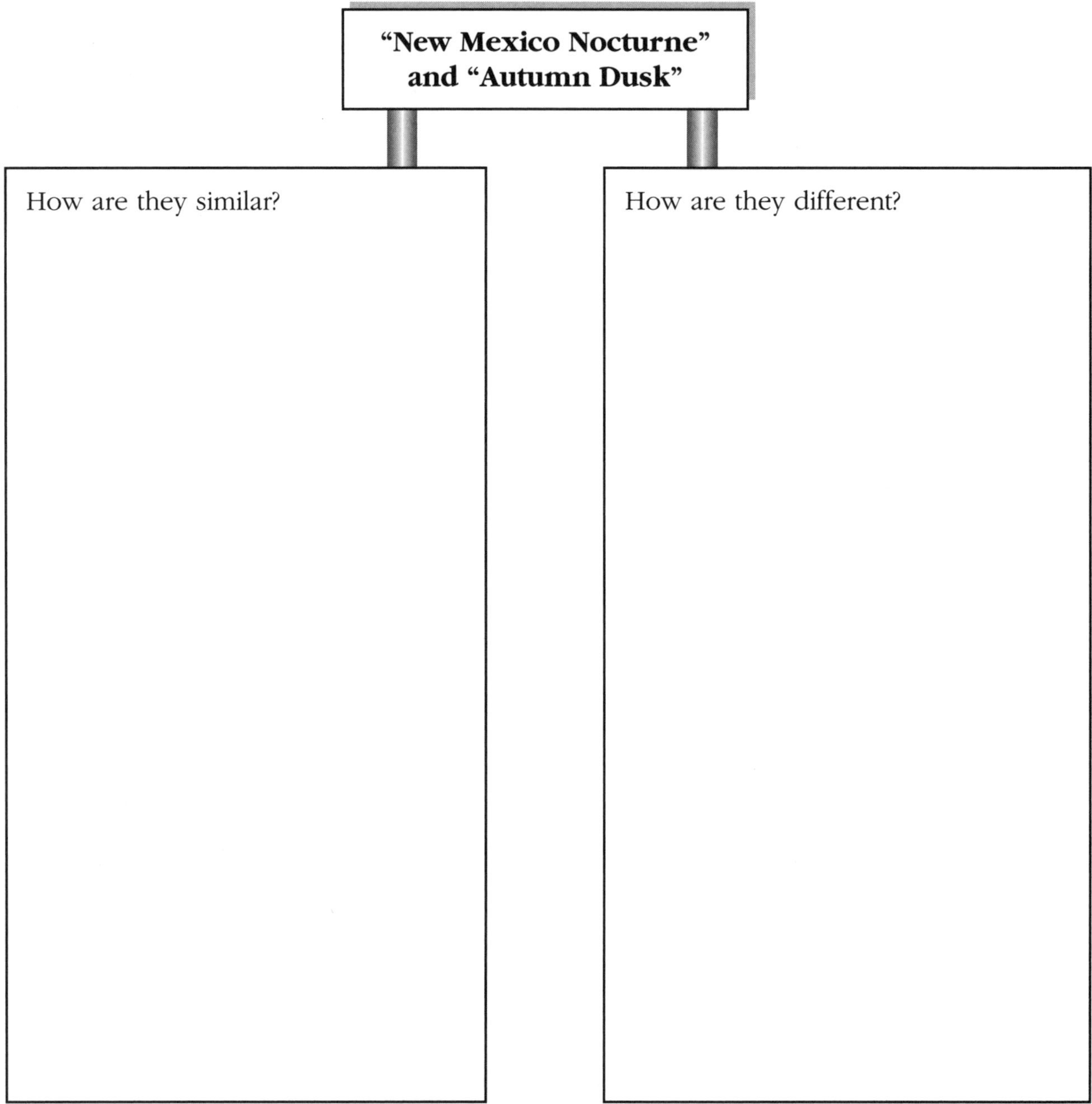

Go on ➤

2. Now write an essay comparing and contrasting the two poems. Use the information you listed on the chart to help you organize your ideas.

   A good way to begin your essay is to point out an obvious similarity. Both poems, for example, were written by Manuela Williams Crosno.

"New Mexico Nocturne" and "Autumn Dusk"

Go on ➤

3. The word *nocturne* has several meanings. In art, a nocturne is a painting of a night scene. In music, a nocturne is a dreamy melody, appropriate to the evening or night. Explain why the first poem is called "New Mexico Nocturne." In your answer, refer to lines and images from the poem.

4. "New Mexico Nocturne" ends with these words:

> ". . . and from some small peak far below
> a mourning dove flies wingward to the sun."

Reread the lines. Briefly describe the picture that the poet paints. Then tell why you think the poet chose to end the poem this way.

Go on ➤

5. Read the following proverb:

It is better to have loved and lost than never to have loved at all.

Show that Manuela Williams Crosno most likely agreed with this proverb. Refer to material in the biographical sketch and in the poem "Autumn Dusk" to support this point of view.

Be sure to check your writing for correct spelling, capitalization, punctuation, and grammar.

Go on ➤

IV. Study Skills

Reading a map. Below is part of a map of New Mexico. Use the map, the compass points, and the scale to answer the questions that follow. Fill in the circle next to the correct answer.

NEW MEXICO

Go on ➤

1. Manuela Williams Crosno's stories take place in and around Santa Fe, Taos, and Albuquerque. To get to Santa Fe or Taos from Albuquerque, in which direction would you travel?
   Ⓐ northwest
   Ⓑ northeast
   Ⓒ southwest
   Ⓓ southeast

2. What is the capital of New Mexico?
   Ⓐ Albuquerque
   Ⓑ. Taos
   Ⓒ Santa Fe
   Ⓓ Los Alamos

3. About how far is Albuquerque from Santa Fe?
   Ⓐ 10 miles
   Ⓑ 20 miles
   Ⓒ 60 miles
   Ⓓ 150 miles

4. About how many miles would you travel to get to Taos from Santa Fe?
   Ⓐ 20 miles
   Ⓑ 70 miles
   Ⓒ 150 miles
   Ⓓ 200 miles

5. In which direction would you travel to get to the Acoma Pueblo from Albuquerque?
   Ⓐ northeast
   Ⓑ northwest
   Ⓒ southeast
   Ⓓ south

6. What is the name of the river that flows through New Mexico?
   Ⓐ White Sands River
   Ⓑ Bandelier River
   Ⓒ Rio Grande
   Ⓓ Alamogordo River

7. Which one of the following is a national monument?
   Ⓐ Chaco Canyon
   Ⓑ Pueblo de Taos
   Ⓒ Socorro
   Ⓓ Santa Fe Ski Basin

8. In which direction would you travel to get to Las Cruces from Albuquerque?
   Ⓐ south
   Ⓑ north
   Ⓒ east
   Ⓓ west

DIRECTIONS
Read the article. Then answer the questions that follow.

The Key to Security? It's a Lock!

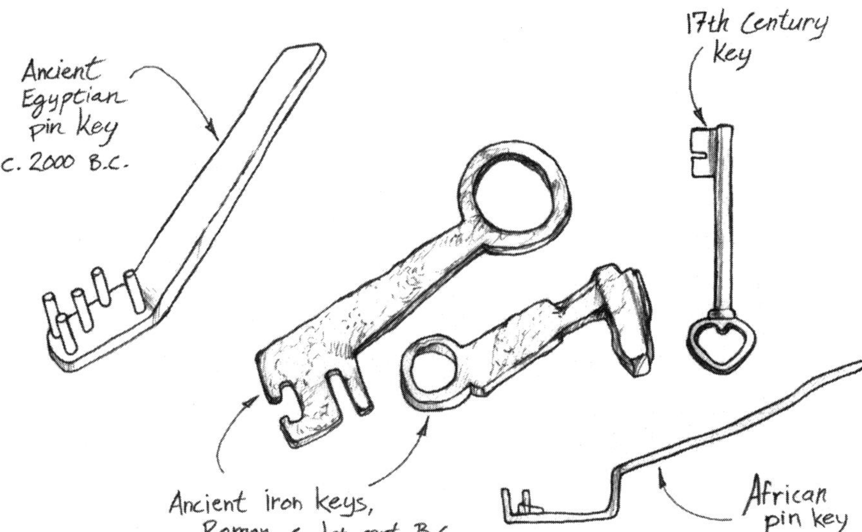

If you dig into your pocket or purse right now, chances are you'll find something that was invented many thousands of years ago. No, it's not a pen—pens go back only as far as Roman times to the year A.D. 100 or so. It's not your spare change either—historians say that the first coins were produced in the country of Lydia (about where Turkey is today) in the sixth century B.C.

Still don't know? The answer is easy—it's the house key!

Approximately 4,000 years ago, ancient Egyptians became the first people to use locks and keys to protect their possessions. Of course, those Egyptian keys bore little resemblance to modern keys, and they would not be very practical to use today. To begin with, they would be too awkward and difficult to carry. They were two to three feet long and carved out of very heavy wood. Picture a huge toothbrush with several large wooden pegs where the bristles would be—that's what an ancient Egyptian key looked like.

Needless to say, there were some disadvantages to this key. Obviously, its size made it cumbersome to carry. Another problem was that it was difficult to hide the key, so a determined and cunning thief could duplicate the original and use the copy to open the lock.

The ancient Greeks designed a key that was smaller and lighter than the Egyptian key. However, the Greek key had a round blade that was about a foot long, so it wasn't exactly a key you could carry around very easily. This did not bother the ancient Greeks because

---

For additional exercises and a story in which a special lock plays a significant role in the plot, see "A Retrieved Reformation" in *More Conflicts* in *Goodman's Five-Star Stories,* Level H.

their keys were not only used to protect their homes but also served as symbols of status and wealth. Their keys had long handles that were often beautifully carved out of ivory or decorated with solid gold.

The ancient Romans were the first to invent the kind of key you would recognize today. Their keys were made of metal, either iron or bronze, and were small enough to fit fairly comfortably in the hand. Unlike earlier keys, many Roman keys were made with complicated patterns to thwart thieves who might otherwise attempt to duplicate them.

Roman garments did not have pockets, so keys were specially designed with this in mind. The key had a hole at one end that enabled a person to wear it as a finger ring. This allowed a Roman to show off the beauty and craft of the key's handle, while the key itself was safely hidden away in the wearer's palm.

In Europe during the Middle Ages, locks and keys were commonly used to protect the treasure chests in which noblemen stored their valuables. Sometimes the locks on these chests were ingeniously crafted to inflict severe pain on anyone who tried to pry them open. In one such chest, if a robber attempted to force open the lock, a steel dart was ejected into the intruder's hand.

Another kind of treasure chest was even more perilous. Here is how it worked: If a thief managed to unlock the chest and open its lid, he would discover another lid below. When he raised the handles of the second lid, a set of metal jaws with sharp metal teeth clamped down on his hand. The unfortunate thief, his hand bleeding and crushed, was trapped and unable to get away or to even move very far. This is how we got the expression "caught red-handed."

Another kind of chest was designed to temporarily blind a thief as he attempted to open the lock. When the lock was disturbed, a spray of pepper was ejected into the thief's eyes. His cries of surprise and pain alerted the nearby guards to his presence.

Today, of course, many locks work on the "combination" principle. To open a combination lock, a small wheel must be rotated back and forth to a particular set of numbers. Only the correct combination of numbers will open the lock. Most likely, this is the kind of lock you have on your locker at school or the kind you might use to chain a bicycle. Most combination locks use a single rotating wheel and are quite easy to use.

A far more complicated combination lock is used to protect the most secure room in the world: The vault at Fort Knox, Kentucky.

That vault contains the United States gold reserves—the single largest quantity of gold anywhere.

Fort Knox is guarded by its own formidable army of highly trained soldiers. The fort was constructed using thousands of tons of stone and is reinforced by more than a thousand tons of steel. The entire building is equipped with cameras, which make it impossible for anyone to take a step inside without being seen. The vault's steel door alone weighs 20 tons, and the lock is so complicated that no one individual knows the entire combination.

The lock at Fort Knox is very different from those first Egyptian locks and their wooden keys. Still, the basic principle is the same: People continue to rely on locks to protect the things they value the most.

Go on ➤

I. Reading Comprehension Skills

Fill in the circle next to the correct answer.

1. What is the article mostly about?
   - Ⓐ keys used by the ancient Romans
   - Ⓑ treasure chests in the Middle Ages
   - Ⓒ keys and locks through the years
   - Ⓓ how combination locks work

2. Which sentence is *not* true of ancient Egyptian keys?
   - Ⓐ They were large and heavy.
   - Ⓑ It was almost impossible to make a copy of them.
   - Ⓒ They were awkward to carry.
   - Ⓓ They were difficult to hide.

3. Why were some ancient Greek keys decorated with gold?
   - Ⓐ to make them difficult to duplicate
   - Ⓑ to make them easier to handle
   - Ⓒ to make them easy to identify
   - Ⓓ to suggest that the owner was a person of wealth

4. According to the article, many treasure chests were specially designed to discourage thieves by
   - Ⓐ causing injury to anyone who tried to break into them.
   - Ⓑ setting off a loud siren when they were pried open.
   - Ⓒ containing several locks, each of which required a different key.
   - Ⓓ exploding when they were opened.

5. Since no one person knows the combination to the lock on the vault at Fort Knox, we may infer that
   - Ⓐ the vault has never been opened.
   - Ⓑ there is no need for the fort to be guarded by trained soldiers.
   - Ⓒ the lock uses one rotating wheel.
   - Ⓓ the combination contains a great many numbers.

6. Which one of the following does the article imply?
   - Ⓐ It was foolish of the ancient Greeks to use wooden keys.
   - Ⓑ It is just about impossible to steal gold from Fort Knox.
   - Ⓒ If you had plenty of time, you could figure out the combination to any combination lock.
   - Ⓓ A combination lock is not as effective as a lock and key.

Answers

1.	Ⓐ	Ⓑ	Ⓒ	Ⓓ
2.	Ⓐ	Ⓑ	Ⓒ	Ⓓ
3.	Ⓐ	Ⓑ	Ⓒ	Ⓓ
4.	Ⓐ	Ⓑ	Ⓒ	Ⓓ
5.	Ⓐ	Ⓑ	Ⓒ	Ⓓ
6.	Ⓐ	Ⓑ	Ⓒ	Ⓓ

Go on ➤

7. What is the main point of the article?
   Ⓐ It is impossible to stop thieves if they are determined to steal something.
   Ⓑ Most combination locks do not work well.
   Ⓒ The locks and keys used today are not much better than those used many years ago.
   Ⓓ People have depended on locks for thousands of years.

8. To the ancient Greeks, the key was a symbol of status and riches. The word *status* means
   Ⓐ social standing or wealth.
   Ⓑ protection or defense.
   Ⓒ power or strength.
   Ⓓ fright or fear.

9. Some keys were made with complicated patterns to thwart thieves who might otherwise copy them. The word *thwart* means
   Ⓐ challenge or dare.
   Ⓑ block or prevent.
   Ⓒ amaze or astound.
   Ⓓ encourage or urge on.

10. Fort Knox is guarded by its own formidable army. The word *formidable* means
   Ⓐ small.
   Ⓑ hardworking.
   Ⓒ difficult to defeat.
   Ⓓ highly paid.

Answers

7. Ⓐ Ⓑ Ⓒ Ⓓ
8. Ⓐ Ⓑ Ⓒ Ⓓ
9. Ⓐ Ⓑ Ⓒ Ⓓ
10. Ⓐ Ⓑ Ⓒ Ⓓ

How many questions did you answer correctly? Circle your score below. Then fill in your **Comprehension** score on the **Test-Taker Score Chart** on the inside of the back cover.

Number Correct	1	2	3	4	5	6	7	8	9	10
My Score	10	20	30	40	50	60	70	80	90	100

Go on ➤

II. Mechanics (capitalization, punctuation, the comma, spelling, and grammar)

Fill in the circle next to the correct answer.

1. Which sentence has an error in capitalization?
   Ⓐ The article states that ancient Egyptian keys were two to three feet long.
   Ⓑ Combination locks are often used on lockers in schools.
   Ⓒ In europe during the Middle Ages, valuables were sometimes kept in treasure chests.
   Ⓓ The vault at Fort Knox is guarded by an army of highly trained soldiers.

2. Which sentence has an error in punctuation?
   Ⓐ Ancient Roman garments didnt have pockets.
   Ⓑ When the lock was disturbed, it ejected pepper into the intruder's eyes.
   Ⓒ Kim suddenly cried out, "I've lost my keys!"
   Ⓓ Yes, keys have changed a great deal over the years.

3. Which sentence needs a comma or does not use the comma correctly?
   Ⓐ The ancient Greeks made keys that were smaller, lighter, and more beautiful than previous keys.
   Ⓑ However, old Roman keys had a round blade that was about a foot long.
   Ⓒ Therefore those keys weren't very handy to carry around.
   Ⓓ Is the combination to the vault at Fort Knox very complicated?

4. Which sentence has an error in spelling in the underlined word?
   Ⓐ The main purpose of a lock is to discourage a <u>thief</u>.
   Ⓑ Currently, many locks work on the "combination" <u>principle</u>.
   Ⓒ She carefully unlocked the chest and opened <u>its</u> lid
   Ⓓ We would probably not find ancient locks <u>satisfactary</u> today.

5. Which one of the following has a mistake in grammar?
   Ⓐ Natalia misplaced the key to her car. She went home by taxi.
   Ⓑ Which one of the three locks is the lightest?
   Ⓒ Chang rotated the combination lock, and the door suddenly flew open.
   Ⓓ Some Roman keys could be worn on a finger, many of the keys were very beautiful.

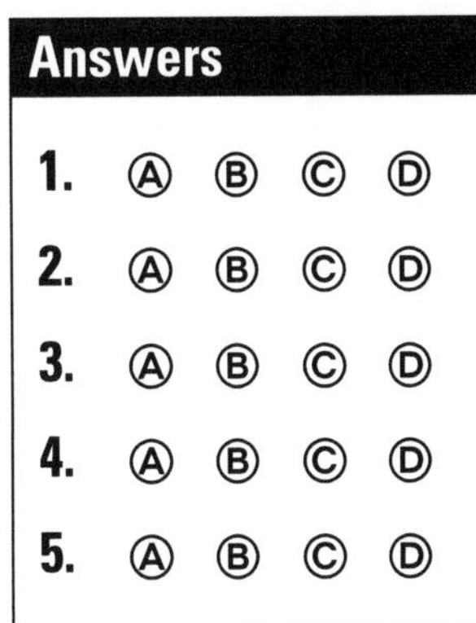
Answers

1. Ⓐ Ⓑ Ⓒ Ⓓ
2. Ⓐ Ⓑ Ⓒ Ⓓ
3. Ⓐ Ⓑ Ⓒ Ⓓ
4. Ⓐ Ⓑ Ⓒ Ⓓ
5. Ⓐ Ⓑ Ⓒ Ⓓ

How many questions did you answer correctly? Circle your score below. Then fill in your **Mechanics** score on the **Test-Taker Score Chart** on the inside of the back cover.

Number Correct	1	2	3	4	5
Your Score	20	40	60	80	100

Go on ➤

III. Writing

Answer the questions that follow. You may look back at the article as often as you wish.

1. A summary briefly provides the main facts in a story or article. Carefully review "The Key to Security? It's a Lock!" Use the outline form below to help you organize the main facts.

I. Ancient Keys

A. Egyptian keys

1. ______________________________

2. ______________________________

B. Greek keys

1. ______________________________

2. ______________________________

3. ______________________________

C. Roman keys

1. ______________________________

2. ______________________________

3. ______________________________

II. Modern Locks and Keys

A. Combination locks

1. ______________________________

2. ______________________________

3. ______________________________

B. Fort Knox

1. ______________________________

2. ______________________________

3. ______________________________

Go on ➤

2. Now use your outline to help you write a summary of "The Key to Security? It's a Lock!"

Be sure to check your writing for correct spelling, capitalization, punctuation, and grammar.

A Summary of "A Key to Security? It's a Lock!"

Go on ➤

3. The article indicates that people rely on locks to protect the things they value the most. What are some of the things you value the most? Are they possessions, or are they personal characteristics, abilities, and skills? Can the most important things you have be locked up with a key? Use the space below to organize your ideas and thoughts about this topic.

Notes

Go on ➤

4. Now use your notes to write an essay about the things you value the most.

Be sure to check your writing for correct spelling, capitalization, punctuation, and grammar.

The Things I Value the Most

Stop